ABDO
Publishing Company

Swimming

MOVE YOUR BODY

A Kid's Guide to Fitness

Buddy BOOKS
Move Your Body

A Buddy Book by **Sarah Tieck**

VISIT US AT
www.abdopublishing.com

Published by ABDO Publishing Company, PO Box 398166, Minneapolis, MN 55439.

Printed in the United States of America, North Mankato, Minnesota.
092012
012013

 PRINTED ON RECYCLED PAPER

Coordinating Series Editor: Rochelle Baltzer
Contributing Editors: Megan M. Gunderson, Marcia Zappa
Graphic Design: Jenny Christensen
Cover Photograph: *Shutterstock*: Ersler Dmitry.
Interior Photographs/Illustrations: *Eighth Street Studio* (p. 26); *Glow Images*: Superstock (p. 13); *iStockphoto*: ©iStockphoto.com/dejanristovski (p. 30), ©iStockphoto.com/ gchutka (p. 25), ©iStockphoto.com/kali9 (p. 29), ©iStockphoto.com/LUGO (p. 23), ©iStockphoto.com/Purdue9394 (p. 7), ©iStockphoto.com/Rubberball (p. 9), ©iStockphoto.com/skynesher (p. 5), ©iStockphoto.com/MarkSwallow (p. 30); *Photo Researchers, Inc.*: Bill Bachmann (p. 21); *Shutterstock*: Allsop (p. 7), leonello calvetti (p. 15), EpicStockMedia (p. 11), Scott Hales (p. 27), Robert Kneschke (p. 19), paulaphoto (p. 17), Andrey Yurlov (p. 15).

Library of Congress Cataloging-in-Publication Data

Tieck, Sarah, 1976-
  Swimming / Sarah Tieck.
    p. cm. -- (Move your body : a kid's guide to fitness)
  ISBN 978-1-61783-564-3
  1. Swimming--Juvenile literature. I. Title.
  GV837.6.T54 2012
  797.2'1--dc23
                          2012025968

Table of Contents

Healthy Living

Your body is amazing! A healthy body helps you feel good and live well. In order to be healthy, you must take care of yourself. One way to do this is to move your body.

Regular movement gives you **energy** and makes you stronger. Many kinds of exercise can help you do this. One fun type of exercise is swimming! Let's learn more about swimming.

Children should get 60 minutes of movement every day. Swimming is a great way to do this!

Swimming 101

Swimmers move their bodies in water. They pull with their hands and arms. They kick with their feet and legs. Together, these movements make up strokes.

Swimmers use strokes to move their bodies through the water. Different strokes help swimmers move fast or slow.

Swimmers may do laps in pools. Or, they may swim outside in lakes or oceans. You may even swim a little as you play in the water!

Teamwork

Swimmers use five basic strokes. These are the breaststroke, the front crawl, the butterfly, the backstroke, and the sidestroke.

Four kicks are part of these strokes. They are the dolphin kick, the breaststroke kick, the flutter kick, and the scissors kick.

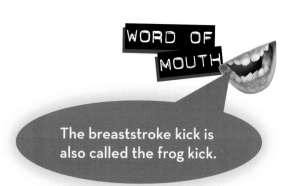

WORD OF MOUTH

The breaststroke kick is also called the frog kick.

The flutter kick is the most popular and easy to learn. Swimmers simply kick one foot up while the other goes down.

Certain kicks are used for each stroke. The breaststroke kick is used for the breaststroke. The dolphin kick is used for the butterfly. The scissors kick is used for the sidestroke. And, the flutter kick is used for the front crawl and backstroke.

The front crawl is one of the most common strokes. Swimmers move their arms in a circle through the water. One hand reaches forward while the other pulls down underwater.

Let's Get Physical

People exercise to stay fit. Regular exercise makes you more **flexible**. It helps you stay at a healthy body weight. And, it helps prevent health problems later in life.

Swimming is a type of **aerobic** exercise. It makes your **lungs** and heart work hard to get your body more **oxygen**. Over time, this strengthens your lungs and heart.

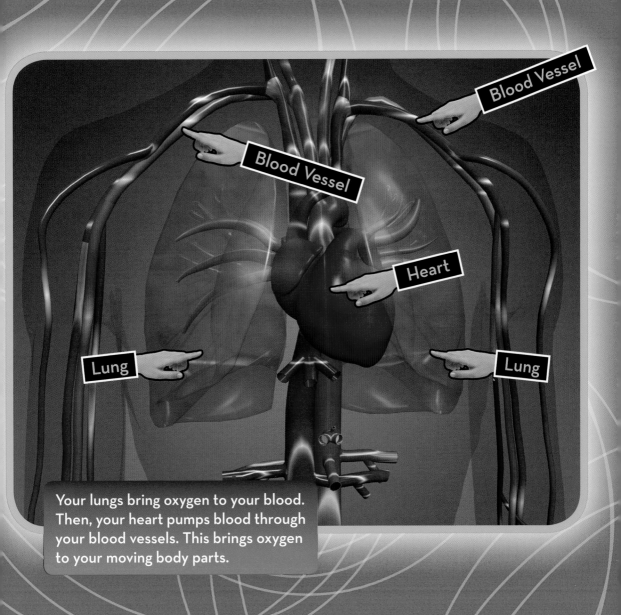

Blood Vessel

Blood Vessel

Heart

Lung

Lung

Your lungs bring oxygen to your blood. Then, your heart pumps blood through your blood vessels. This brings oxygen to your moving body parts.

Swimming also builds your **muscles**. When you do the strokes, you work your arm muscles. And, your body turns slightly. This builds your **abdominal** and back muscles. Kicking works your leg muscles.

Other swimming movements, such as treading water, also strengthen your muscles. Over time, your muscles get stronger. Then, they can move you through the water more easily.

Your upper arm has muscles that move it in different directions. The triceps are on the back of your arm. Your biceps are in front.

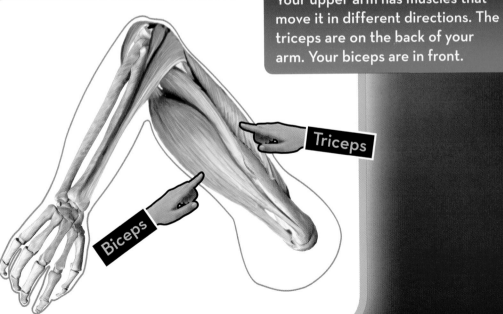

Triceps

Biceps

Gearing Up

To swim, you will wear a swimming suit on your body. Some people wear flippers on their feet. Masks, goggles, nose plugs, and ear plugs can also be helpful.

You might need different types of gear for different types of swimming. A swim cap is helpful for racing. You might wear water shoes for swimming in a lake or ocean.

WORD OF MOUTH

Some racers cover their hair with a swim cap to move faster through the water.

Swimmers often wear goggles to help them see underwater and to protect their eyes.

Ready? Set? Go!

When you start swimming, warm up by doing slow strokes. This prepares your **muscles** to work hard. Cool down by swimming slowly to help keep your muscles from getting sore.

Stretching is an important part of any exercise. Over time, it makes you more **flexible**. This makes it easier for your body to move.

Swimmers often stand in the water to do their stretches.

Play It Safe

Swimming can be unsafe. You could get hurt or even drown. So, it is important to be careful when you swim.

Many children take swimming lessons. They learn basic swimming strokes and water safety. Schools and community groups offer lessons for swimmers of all skill levels.

Taking swimming lessons can help you be safer and stronger in the water.

One way to stay safe is to never swim alone. And, always have an adult watch you. Some places have lifeguards on duty. Be sure to follow their instructions.

Some swimmers use toys and tools to help them swim. These include water wings, kickboards, and life jackets.

WORD OF MOUTH

Many toys, such as water wings, can help you swim. But, they can lose their air. So, don't depend on them to keep you safe.

Life jackets help people be safe in the water. They are important tools for beginning and experienced swimmers.

Look and Learn

When you swim, be aware of your surroundings. Remember to swim where an adult can see you. In a pool, follow the safety rules and look out for other swimmers. Pay attention to how deep or shallow the water is.

Swimming in a natural body of water is different from swimming in pools. There are other things to watch for in lakes, oceans, and rivers. Only swim in safe areas that are clean and clear.

Watch the weather when swimming outdoors. Never swim during a storm or when there's lightning.

WORD OF MOUTH

Rivers, oceans, and lakes can have powerful water. Be aware of waves, currents, and changes in tides. And, follow a lifeguard's instructions about when and where it is safe to swim.

Brain Food

What should you do if you are having trouble in the water?

You can yell for help. But, it is important to know how to stay safe until help arrives. Many people do a type of floating called survival bobbing.

First, you fill your lungs with air. Then, you let your body relax with your face in the water. When you need a breath, you lift your face up. The air in your lungs allows you to float until help arrives.

Is it true that you need to wait 30 minutes after eating to swim?

No. At one time, people believed you could not swim while **digesting** food. That's because your body pumps extra blood to your stomach after you eat. But, it still has enough blood to help move your arms and legs, too.

Are there more than five swimming strokes?

Yes, there are many other strokes. A well-known stroke is the dog paddle. Another is the elementary backstroke. These strokes are some of the first ones many people learn.

Choose to Move

Remember that swimming is a type of fitness that makes your body stronger. Fitness is an important part of a healthy life. Swim as often as you can! Each positive choice you make will help you stay healthy.

Swimming is good for your body.
Splashing in the cool water is fun, too!

STAY SAFE

✔ Don't chew gum or eat while swimming. You could choke.

✔ Wear water-resistant sunscreen when you swim outside.

EAT RIGHT

✔ Lean **proteins** are one food that can help improve your swimming. They build **muscle**. Chicken and low-fat milk are both lean proteins.

✔ Be sure to drink water before and after swimming.

MOVE MORE

✔ Set a **goal** to improve your swimming. Distance or time are ways to measure progress.

✔ Take a break while swimming to check your heart rate. Touch the inside of your wrist. Then, count the pulses in one minute.

Important Words

abdominal relating to the part of the body between the chest and the hips.

aerobic (ehr-OH-bihk) relating to exercise that increases oxygen in the body and makes the heart better able to use oxygen.

digest (deye-JEHST) to break down food into parts small enough for the body to use.

energy (EH-nuhr-jee) the power or ability to do things.

flexible able to bend or move easily.

goal something that a person works to reach or complete.

lungs body parts that help the body breathe.

muscle (MUH-suhl) body tissue, or layers of cells, that helps move the body.

oxygen (AHK-sih-juhn) a colorless gas that humans and animals need to breathe.

protein (PROH-teen) an important part of the diet of all animals.

Web Sites

To learn more about swimming, visit ABDO Publishing Company online. Web sites about swimming are featured on our Book Links page. These links are routinely monitored and updated to provide the most current information available.

www.abdopublishing.com

Index